Original title:
Coral Reef Chronicles

Copyright © 2025 Creative Arts Management OÜ
All rights reserved.

Author: Dean Whitmore
ISBN HARDBACK: 978-1-80587-299-3
ISBN PAPERBACK: 978-1-80587-769-1

The Unseen Evolution of the Deep

Beneath the waves where creatures twirl,
A clownfish lost in quite a swirl.
He's got no map, just a big old grin,
Swimming in circles, can't find his kin.

A turtle once pondered, in need of snacks,
Should he munch on seaweed or some fishy cracks?
With garlic bread dreams, he chased a shrimp,
But ended up stuck in a big sea blimp.

With jellyfish dancing, all floaty and grand,
They mistakenly tickled a passing sand.
The sand yelled back, "Hey, that's not fair!
You don't see me dancing with my sunburned flare!"

A crab in a tux, with a stylish pinch,
Went to a party, said, "I'll make them flinch!"
He waltzed with a starfish, both prancing about,
Until they got tangled, oh what a clout!

As waves whisper tales of the curious sea,
Join the fishy revels, come dance with glee.
In the deep's shadows, laughter will bloom,
With each silly creature crafting the room!

The Language of Shells

The shells converse with style,
With whispers of the sea,
They giggle, they chortle,
As if they're having tea.

A conch shared a pun,
To a starfish in a hat,
'Why don't clams get lost?
They always know where they're at!'

Journeys of the Sea Snails

The sea snails roll and glide,
In their homes all packed tight,
They travel super slow,
But they're quite a sight!

'Why rush?' said a wise one,
As he munched on some kelp,
'Life's a leisurely race,
Just go with the yelp!'

The Enchanted Sea

In waters that shimmer bright,
A sponge danced with glee,
'Every fish here is a star,
In my underwater spree!'

With bubbles of laughter,
The octopus did twirl,
Said, 'Can anyone keep up?
I'm a ten-armed whirl!'

Legends of the Lost Reefs

There lives a fish quite grand,
With tales of the deep,
He claims he once swam,
Where mermaids wouldn't sleep.

His friends roll their eyes,
'Oh, here we go again!
Next he'll claim he met,
A giant octopus named Ken!'

Guardians of the Sea Floor

A crab with a hat, all dapper and neat,
Waves to a fish, who's lost both her feet.
They gather their friends for a dance on the sand,
With jellyfish twirlers lending a hand.

The octopus juggles with shells and a shoe,
A dolphin does cartwheels, oh what a view!
With laughter and splashes, the ocean they cheer,
They plan the next party—who'll bring the shrimp beer?

Painted Palaces Underwater

A pufferfish blows up, looking quite wide,
"It's my new look!" he grins, full of pride.
Starfish giggle and roll on the floor,
While a sea turtle snoozes, dreaming of more.

Clownfish in costumes, oh what a sight,
In bubbles of laughter, all day and all night.
The sea cucumbers dance, quite out of sync,
They trip over turtles, oh what a wink!

Cradles of Color

In gardens of kelp, where the fish love to hide,
A shrimp throws a party—"Come join!" he cried.
The anemone giggles, with friends all around,
They paint all the rocks, making joy abound.

A lobster in glasses declaring a toast,
"We're the best pals! Let's party the most!"
With seaweed confetti fluttering high,
"Next round of shells is on me!" he'll cry.

Swaying with the Sea Grass

Sea horses glide like they're on a parade,
Ballet with bubbles, an elegant trade.
The sea urchins laugh, "Look, we've found our groove!"
They sway and they twist, putting on a move.

With crabs doing handstands, oh what a scene,
A clownfish jokes, "Hey, have you seen my jean?"
Amidst all this fun, the ocean's alive,
Where silliness reigns, and joy will survive.

Echoes of the Ocean Floor

Bubbles rise in a giddy spree,
Fish all giggle, they swim with glee.
Crabs in hats do a silly dance,
While starfish wink and take a chance.

An octopus plays a wild kazoo,
As seahorses twirl in a parade too.
They flaunt their colors, a vibrant show,
While the clams clap shells, in a rhythmic flow.

Dance of the Anemones

Twisting and turning, they sway in delight,
With ticklish fingers that dance through the night.
A clownfish giggles, with spots of bright red,
While the anemones wiggle, 'You're ticklish!' they said.

Jellyfish bob and bubble with pride,
As plankton spin round in the joyous tide.
They join in the fun, twirling without care,
Underwater laughter fills the salty air.

Secrets of the Undercurrent

Turtles tell tales of drama and strife,
Of a crab that once stole a fish's wife.
A dolphin leaps high, mimicking the sun,
And the blowfish puffs up, thinking it's fun.

A puffer plays peek-a-boo, quite bold,
While a hidden treasure is waiting to be sold.
But the sea urchins chuckle, 'Not so fast, my friend!'
For they all know that games never end.

Adventures in the Abyss

Deep in the shadows where no light can reach,
A goblin shark whispers, 'Hey, want a peach?'
While anglerfish giggle, their lanterns aglow,
They throw a surprise party, oh what a show!

With squid juggling pearls and posh jelly jelly,
The deep-sea duo dance, all wobbly and smelly.
They toast with the bubbles, a fizzy delight,
In the depths of the ocean, they partied all night.

Reflections in Aquamarine

In the depths where fish do prance,
A seahorse spins, he loves to dance.
An octopus in stylish shades,
Sneaks up on crabs, then swiftly fades.

The clownfish laughs, puts on a show,
Says, 'Can you believe I still can glow?'
Turtles glide with such cool ease,
While bragging about their bumpy knees.

A parrotfish munches on some rock,
Sings, 'It's five o'clock! Let's take stock!'
A starfish yawned, said with a sigh,
'It's hard to be famous when you're flat as pie!'

The waters sparkle, the fun's alive,
In this blue world, fish freely thrive.
So let's dive deep and make a splash,
With giggles and bubbles, we'll make a dash!

Odyssey of the Once-Wild Ocean

A dolphin named Phil thought he could fly,
Jumped out the waves, kissed the sky goodbye.
He belly-flopped into a jelly's embrace,
Said, 'This wasn't quite my dream of space.'

The crabs throw a party, dance in a line,
While saying, 'Our dance moves are just divine!'
But every few steps, they change their mind,
And end up sideways—their style defined.

A whale with a hat sings opera each night,
His fishy fans cheer, 'Oh, what a sight!'
With bubbles to blow and songs so grand,
The ocean's stage is a one-man band.

They hold a contest for the best joke,
A fish tells a tale that makes all hearts choke.
Laughter erupts under the moonlit sun,
In this wild ocean, there's always fun!

Whispers Beneath the Waves

In underwater halls, where secrets creep,
A crab whispers low, 'I don't like sleep!'
He taps a conch, dreaming of fame,
Hoping his snips will make him a name.

A pufferfish pouted, feeling so grand,
Declared, 'I know how to make a band!'
He puffed up a trumpet, gave it a blow,
The bass fish jumped, said, 'Go with the flow!'

The seaweed sways with stories untold,
Of fish that wear socks, proud and bold.
A mermaid grins, with pearls in her hair,
Says, 'Who needs shoes? We're quite debonair!'

Bubbles of laughter float through the scene,
In the whispers below, where nobody's mean.
With fishy shenanigans and all the glee,
Life in the water is quite a jubilee!

The Colorful Underworld

In a world painted bright, where the sea critters dwell,
A clownfish named Chuck discovered a shell.
He squeaked, 'What a find! It's a treasure galore!'
'Turns out it's just a lost shoe from the shore!'

Anemones sway, with a tickle and tease,
While fish take a nap in the soft sea breeze.
But wait, oh dear! A crab seeks revenge,
Biting the toes of a fish in the den.

A flamboyant squid puts on a grand show,
With colors that swirl, putting on a glow.
He twirled and he spun, oh what a delight,
While the seabed critters gasped in pure fright.

Underwater art, with laughter and fun,
As creatures assemble, all gathered as one.
In this colorful world, joy does abound,
In the depths of the sea, sweet amusement is found!

Serendipitous Sea Selections

In a school of fish, a dance so bold,
They wiggle and jiggle, if truth be told.
One fish lost its specs, quite the sight,
Now it bumps into rocks, oh what a fright!

A lobster in shades, living the dream,
Sipping seaweed smoothies, oh what a theme!
A seahorse prancing, trying to glide,
But it trips on a wave, with jellyfish pride!

A clam that tells jokes, never a bore,
Its pearls of wisdom leave us wanting more.
With a wink and a grin, it shares the scoop,
While starfish laugh, joining the troop!

So come take a dip, don't be shy,
In this underwater circus, oh my oh my!
The fish are all laughing, the laughs are free,
In the depths of the ocean, it's the place to be!

Constellations of Corals

Beneath the waves, a colorful show,
Where coral bumps into algae, nice to know.
A parrotfish munches, don't mind the flair,
While a clownfish giggles, curls up in its lair!

Octopuses juggle, they've got quite the flair,
Throwing pebbles and shells like they just don't care.
A turtle's slow dance sparks fits of glee,
While a fish in a top hat yells, "Look at me!"

The bubbles rise up, like laughter in the air,
As sea cucumbers whisper, "Life's not so rare."
Eels make their entrance, with a slithery style,
While crabs do the cha-cha, with shells that beguile!

So come take a glimpse, at this ghostly delight,
Where every wiggle and giggle feels just right.
In the realms of the blues, life dances anew,
With constellations of corals, winking at you!

Underwater Epiphanies

A fish with a feather, oh what a sight,
Hoping to fly in the moonlight.
It flaps and it flops, but to no avail,
Dreams of the sky, in a fishy tale!

Anemones sigh, they can't catch a break,
The clownfish tells jokes, they start to quake.
A dolphin appears, with a grin so wide,
Now they're all giggling, tucked in the tide!

A hermit crab's house is too big for his feet,
He drags it around, now isn't that sweet?
A pufferfish grins, puffed up with glee,
Saying "Life's just a float, come laugh with me!"

So sink down below, past the gentle sway,
In this underwater world, we'll frolic and play.
With shells full of stories and bubbles that gleam,
Life's a great splash, or at least it seems!

Wonders of the Aquatic Canopy

In the deepest blue, where wonders reside,
A fish in a tux waits for the tide.
With seahorses sipping on sea sponge shakes,
And jellyfish jingling, oh what fun makes!

A unicorn fish, with a laugh oh so bright,
Knows all the gossip from morning to night.
While munching on algae, it spills the tea,
About a grouper who thinks he's a celebrity!

Starfish lay back, counting the tides,
As a mermaid joins in with glittery rides.
An octopus practices a stand-up act,
With eight arms of punchlines, it's quite a fact!

So dive into laughter, come swim with the crew,
Where bubbles are dreams, and the sea sparkles too.
In the wonders below, we'll frolic with glee,
In the aquatic canopy, just you wait and see!

Watercolor Dreams of Divers

Bubbles burst like tiny balloons,
Fins flapping in offbeat tunes.
Goggles fogged, they can't see right,
Chasing fish that dart from sight.

With a splash and a hearty dive,
Expecting grace but feeling jive.
The seaweed tickles as they sway,
While crabs dance in a clumsy ballet.

A turtle laughs, he's just so cool,
While divers fumble like they're in school.
Kicking up sand in a swirling fray,
Getting lost in the game they play.

Glimpses of colors all around,
With giggles that echo, joyful sound.
Their underwater world, a funny craze,
In watercolor dreams, they swim and play.

Lullabies of the Open Ocean

Waves whisper secrets in tones so sweet,
As sailors snore, and fish dance on feet.
Starfish prance to lullabies sung,
While the sea sings softly, forever young.

A seagull squawks, steals a snack,
Fishermen chuckle, 'Hey, get back!'
Sleeping crabs dream of sandy bliss,
While dolphins giggle in a frothy mist.

Octopus cooks, a chef with flair,
Flipping shells in the ocean air.
Mussels hum tunes in a clammy choir,
Lullabies play as they never tire.

The moonlight dances on silken waves,
Nature's orchestra, it's what she gave.
Dreams float by in a salty breeze,
As the ocean rocks, putting hearts at ease.

Kaleidoscope of Life

A fish in a tux, how fancy indeed,
With scales that shimmer, they're born to lead.
A parrotfish chomps, nibbling on coral,
As a clownfish giggles, 'Life's a moral!'

Jellyfish float, like balloons of glee,
Pulsing rhythms in a sea that's free.
Crabs compete in a sideways race,
Each pinch and poke a humorous chase.

Seahorses dance, a bizarre duet,
In gowns of seaweed, don't you forget.
A nudibranch flaunts its bright attire,
While under the waves, they never tire.

In this vibrant world, colors collide,
Where laughter and playfulness never hide.
Life's a funny show, just take a glance,
In the kaleidoscope, we all prance.

Chasing the Crystal Current

In a bubble of laughter, they splash through blue,
Chasing the current, what a wacky crew!
Waves tickle noses and fins flap loud,
As fish giggle back, oh, aren't they proud?

Who knew the ocean's such a funny place?
With sea cucumbers sharing space.
A starfish worries, 'Am I a star?'
While squid do flips, 'Oh, how bizarre!'

Snorkelers trip over sea urchin spikes,
Swirling underwater like wild bikes.
They point to a manatee munching a snack,
And laugh as it glances, 'Just let me relax!'

Chasing the current, laughter cascades,
In the ballet of bubbles, where joy pervades.
A watery tale where fun takes the lead,
In this crystal dance, hearts intercede.

Medleys of Marine Melody

Bubbles rise in guppy dreams,
While fish wear hats and play with beams.
A crab tap dances on the sand,
With seaweed fans in each small hand.

Octopus is quite the chef,
Serving sushi—oops, my left!
The shrimp all laugh, a jolly sight,
As dolphins join to dance with might.

Starfish star in a rock band,
Jellyfish glow, do you understand?
With every wave, the tunes do blend,
Each splash and giggle is our trend.

So dive right in, the water's fine,
With finned friends, we toast with brine.
The ocean hums a rhythmic jest,
In this madcap place, we find our best.

Driftwood Diaries

The driftwood logs for gossip's scene,
Whale tales twisting, fishy and mean.
A seagull squawks, makes quite the fuss,
As everyone stares at the old sea bus.

Anemones wear polka dot bows,
While clownfish tell jokes—everyone knows!
A sea turtle yawns, then flips with grace,
Belly laughs echo in this wild place.

The hermit crabs trade shells on the sly,
One huge shell makes a crab cry,
"I have no space!" He screams with flair,
While shrimp all snicker, tangled in hair.

All aboard for a ride on this whim,
Life's a splash—try not to swim!
With silly thoughts beneath the tide,
Together we laugh, side by side.

The Siren's Silent Symphony

A siren hums without a care,
Her underwater concert's quite rare.
But fish swim by, too busy to stay,
"Not in the mood!" they shout and play.

Sea cucumbers march to the beat,
With sea urchins tapping little feet.
The conch shell blows, but who can hear?
With all this noise, it's just not clear.

Scallops clap like they're at a show,
While turtles groove moving slow.
Hiding from tunes—what a place to be,
In a concert where no one's free!

So join the fun, let melodies flow,
In the sea where laughter overly grows.
A silent night with fishes in sync,
Maybe it's time for a snack and a drink!

Celestial Seas

Twinkling stars in the ocean deep,
Fish form constellations as they leap.
A moonfish grins from a silver tide,
While crabs debate, on whom to bide.

The seahorses hold a space parade,
Each one dressed in glittering jade.
Jellyfish float like balloons so bright,
Casting shadows in the starlit night.

Turtles draw maps with a fin and a shell,
Saying, "To the Milky Way, let's sail!"
Starfish look puzzled, tracing their rays,
As fish spin tales in their swimming ways.

Under these stars, laughter's the key,
With every splash, we sing with glee.
So dance around, and let's take flight,
In celestial seas, all feels so right!

Whispers of the Tides

In the sea where fish gossip and play,
A starfish claims it's a bright sunny day.
But the octopus winks with ink in its pen,
Saying, "Let's dance, my slippery friend!"

The seahorse pranced in a wavy line,
While the clam just sighed, "Oh, this is divine!"
The jellyfish floated with a laugh and a spin,
'Cause with no legs to trip, it can always win!

A crab in a tuxedo, a real snazzy sight,
Clapping its claws, throwing quite the delight!
While the fish all gathered, calling it grand,
"Let's throw a party, isn't this planned?"

So in bubbles and giggles, their troubles dissolve,
In the depths of the ocean, great fun to evolve.

Beneath the Surface

Under the waves where the seaweed sways,
A parrotfish munches on coral buffet.
It chews and it munches, oh what a show,
"Hey, who ordered this salad?" it seems to crow!

The shrimp threw a bash, with dancing galore,
"Come join us, my friends, just ignore the floor!"
But the lobster perched proudly, refusing to groove,
Said, "I'm not a dancer, I'm here to approve!"

A dolphin named Dave had a joke quite profound,
"Why don't we ever see a fish wearing a crown?"
With laughter echoing, the sardines in glee,
"Because fish have no heads, can't you see?"

So beneath the surface, where laughter's a blast,
Each fin and each flipper knows how to have a blast!

Colors of the Deep

In the deep blue sea, colors whirl and twirl,
The clownfish laughs, giving bubbles a whirl.
"I'm orange and white, just a stroke of luck,
Watch out for the blennies, they're sly little mucks!"

The angelfish flutters with shimmering scales,
Flaunting its beauty as it tells grand tales.
"Did you hear the one 'bout the mermaid's new dress?
It was made from the seaweed, I must confess!"

A worsted old turtle with sunken old eyes,
Mumbles of treasure, oh how time flies!
While the sea cucumbers roll by with a shrug,
"Life's better in colors, just give it a hug!"

So in the great depths where the bright colors gleam,
A playful adventure swims far like a dream.

Guardians of the Lagoon

In the calm of the lagoon, where the water is clear,
The guardians gather, bringing laughter and cheer.
A lionfish strutted, proud and so sleek,
While the stingray just giggled, thinking it chic!

The anglefish whispered, "What's the latest scoop?
Did you see the new fish at the coral fish group?"
But the pufferfish grinned, full of wise little glee,
"Don't puff up too much, or you'll scare the sea!"

With turtles as bouncers, they kept it all fun,
"Only funny fish allowed, now isn't that fun?"
With bubbles and laughter, the songs floated high,
As the fish spun around, oh so spry!

So guardians of laughter, protectors of jest,
In the lagoon of joy, they truly are blessed.

Glimmers in the Aquamarine

Bubbling fish with silly grins,
Swirling tales in watery spins,
A hermit crab in shoes too tight,
Stomping 'round, what a silly sight!

An octopus with ink in hand,
Writes poems on the seaweed strand,
While snails on surfboards glide with glee,
Surfing waves in the sparkling sea!

A clownfish juggling with a pearl,
Twirls and giggles, what a whirl!
Turtles dance with fins so spry,
As bubbles float up to the sky!

And all around, colors collide,
In this party where fish reside,
Each splash a giggle, every splash a cheer,
In waters filled with joy and beer!

Reflections of the Vibrant Blue

A pufferfish in polka dots,
Tries to fit in a tiny spot,
With every wiggle, what a squeeze,
He bounces back like a slight breeze!

A parrotfish that loves to chew,
On coral treats, who knew, who knew?
He sings to friends, makes quite the fuss,
With a voice like a rusty bus!

Dancing eels in dopey hats,
Invite the crabs for silly chats,
Each wave a laugh, no time to frown,
Sea life's a joke, no room for down!

Oh, how the jellyfish float around,
In rhythm and rhyme, they bounce, they bound,
With twinkling lights, it's quite the view,
In shades of laughter, bright and blue!

The Submerged Symphony

A turtle strums on seaweed strings,
Creating tunes that make fish sing,
A seahorse dances with finesse,
In this underwater loveliness!

Clams go "clap", while fish do hop,
The ocean floor becomes a shop,
Where laughter rings and bubbles burst,
In a concert where none are cursed!

Anemones sway in the beat,
Inviting all for a silly seat,
With sea stars twinkling in delight,
The ocean's music is outta sight!

As waves crash down and laughter flies,
Moments captured beneath the skies,
A hilarious tune, a joyful spree,
Where every giggle floats free!

Voice of the Deep

A blubbery whale with a huge low sigh,
Whispers secrets as minnows fly,
"Let's play hide and seek," he calls,
While the shyest fish behind coral walls!

A dolphin flips with silly grace,
With a splash, he shows his face,
"Catch me if you can," he shouts,
As fish chase dreams and twist about!

A grouper grumbles, "This is my rock!"
While snorting sea cows munch and talk,
Who knew the depths would hold such fun,
In every ray of the warm sun?

With sea turtles spinning, everyone cheers,
Echoes of laughter fill the years,
No worries bubbled, just smiles so wide,
In the voice of the depths, there's joy, there's pride!

Currents of Vibrancy

In the sea where the fish wear hats,
The clownfish laugh at all the spats.
The sea turtles groove to the tunes,
While jellyfish dance under the moons.

A shrimp tells jokes, he's quite the pro,
With a pinch of salt and a dash of glow.
The starfish clap with their five small hands,
As the hermit crab forms a band with sands.

The parrotfish munch on vibrant snacks,
Swapping stories in colorful packs.
A dolphin whistles, "What a show!"
As the sea anemone steals the glow!

Down in the depths where the colors pop,
The sea's a party, never a stop.
Everyone's laughing, what a delight,
In this underwater carnival bright!

Guardians of the Reef

The fish in suits are quite the sight,
With tiny ties, they're ready to fight.
The crab's a lawyer, sharp and shrewd,
In the court of shells, he's oh-so-mood.

The angelfish patrols with glee,
Saying, "No pollution here, not on my spree!"
The sea horse whispers, "Don't you dare!"
As they dance around without a care.

A turtle yells, "Stop! That's not nice!"
To the fish who thought they could entice.
With a flip and a splash, they take a stand,
Guardians of laughter in this underwater land.

So if you swim by, wear a big grin,
Join their antics, let the fun begin.
For beneath the waves, with a joyful cheer,
The guardians laugh and spread good cheer!

A Diary in Seafoam

Dear Diary, today I had a thought,
A crab on the run, my lunch has been caught!
The fish swam by with a cheeky grin,
I think they know where all the snacks have been.

I saw a mermaid with hair made of kelp,
She sang to the waves, gave the ocean a yelp.
A dolphin flipped, and startled a ray,
While a starfish was napping, just snoozing away.

Oh, the octopus tried to tickle my toes,
But his eight arms tangled like wild disco flows.
The sea cucumbers chuckled in glee,
As I scribbled my thoughts in the soft sea debris.

Tomorrow I'll swim where the bubbles blow,
Perhaps find a treasure, who knows where it'll go?
In my seafoam diary, adventures await,
Here in the depths, life is simply great!

The Plight of the Polyp

Oh little polyp, why the frown?
Is it the seaweed that weighs you down?
You dream of jelly with colors so bright,
But your taco shells are a hit or a fright!

You invite the fish for a feast divine,
But they swim in and out, saying, "Not this time!"
The blennies just giggle while munching on grass,
Leaving you lonely while they pass.

You try your best to look freshly spruced,
But the tides are rough, and you feel no use.
"Don't be shy!" cheer the sneaky sea snails,
"You'll find your groove, just follow our trails!"

So little polyp, raise that smile,
With each tide gone, there's endless style.
For under the waves, the fun's never late,
Embrace the currents and celebrate fate!

Palette of the Ocean

In a world painted blue, bright and bold,
Sea creatures laugh, or so I'm told.
Rainbow fish flaunt their vibrant hues,
Wearing fins like designer shoes.

A turtle in shades, all snazzy and neat,
Waddles around on his flippered feet.
He rolls past crabs who just can't compete,
In this fashion show that can't be beat!

Eels with their stripes, a stylish affair,
Dance through the waters without a care.
Each splash of color, a wacky delight,
Making waves in the broad daylight!

So dive into laughter, let colors ignite,
The ocean's humor is truly a sight.
With every fins' flick and every fish wink,
At the sea's vibrant art, you'll pause and think!

Beneath Blushing Waves

Under the waves where giggles reside,
Fish tell tales with nowhere to hide.
Starfish compete in a friendly race,
While octopuses play in an inky embrace.

Clownfish joke with their comical spouts,
"Why did the shrimp dance? It had no doubts!"
Seahorses giggle, tails intertwined,
In a jolly embrace, perfectly aligned.

A whale's deep laughter vibrates through the sea,
Echoing joy for all fish to be free.
Anemones dance, swaying with glee,
Celebrating life, oh so carefree!

So plunge down below where the light's not so bright,
And join in the fun, it's sure to delight.
In this world of wonders, so wet and so wild,
Silly fish stories will leave you beguiled!

Bioluminescence and Beyond

In the depths where the dark fish glow,
A disco party begins, don't you know?
With neon lights that flicker and play,
They boogie and shine in a dazzling display.

Jellyfish float like lanterns in flight,
Waving their arms, oh what a sight!
A party so bright, it's hard to believe,
Even crabs try to dance, with a pinch and a heave!

Squids make fireworks with ink in the night,
Painting the ocean in colors so bright.
But watch your toes, for a clam might just pop,
In this jelly-rave world, groove till you drop!

Dive into the glow, let your worries all fade,
The ocean's a stage where no one's afraid.
Join the fish fest, let your laughter resound,
In this luminescent party, joy knows no bound!

The Secret Life of Fish

Fish have secrets, just you wait and see,
Like how they gossip about you and me.
"Did you hear about the shrimp with no pants?
He's too shy to join our undersea dance!"

With bubbles and swirls, they chat all day,
Passing on tales in their fishy way.
"Remember the octopus who juggled for laughs?
He got all the snails to join in for half!"

At night they gather, no humans in sight,
Throwing a bash under the moon's gentle light.
They play truth or dare, with a splash and a wiggle,
Making the seahorse do a silly little giggle.

So next time you swim where the fish like to play,
Remember their laughter, their secrets at bay.
For even beneath waves, joy can be found,
In the hilarity of fish, oh so profound!

Chaotic Harmony of the Tides

Bubbles rise like giggling fish,
In oceans where the pranks are swish.
A clownfish juggling, quite the show,
While seaweed dances, to and fro.

The octopus wears a funky hat,
Winking as he chases a gnat.
Starfish flipping in a bold ballet,
While crabs hold parties at the bay.

Turtles racing down the lane,
With swim trunks on, they can't complain.
As dolphins dive and do a spin,
The sea's a circus, shells tucked in!

A seahorse struts in a bright parade,
With shimmering scales, he's never frayed.
In this wild world, they laugh and jest,
In watery realms, they smile the best.

Refugia of Resilience

Anemones hide in their cozy nook,
As fish come to chat, with their funny look.
The parrotfish munches, bright and spry,
Telling tales of the sea sponge, oh my!

A hermit crab swaps shells with flair,
Like fashion shows, they don't care.
With tangled nets of laughter and cheer,
These ocean dwellers hold nothing dear.

Sea turtles giggle while flipping shells,
In this refuge, where everything gels.
A barracuda's chasing after a shoe,
Oops! Just a sock, but what can you do?

In pockets of fun where the sea stars shine,
Every wave brings a joke divine.
They wave their fins and do a cheer,
In this wacky world, there's nothing to fear!

Threads of Life Entrapped

A crab gets caught in a tangle of weeds,
Screaming for help, oh, how funny he pleads!
Fish are laughing, bubbles do burst,
In their tangled web, who knows who's first?

The sea cucumbers roll with glee,
While the jellyfish float, so carefree.
Caught in their dance, they wobble and sway,
In the tangled threads, they groove all day.

A sea urchin prods with disguised flair,
"Don't poke the blob, it's got more to share!"
As sea slugs slide on a slippery plot,
All tangled together, but it's quite the hot spot.

With laughter and gaffes, they waddle along,
In the fabric of fun, they all belong.
In this chaos, life finds its way,
With friends all round, it's a wild display!

Tales of Survival in the Abyss

In the deep blue, where the funny fish dive,
They swap their stories, keeping hope alive.
A flounder tells of a close escape,
From a hungry angler, dressed in a cape!

A pufferfish boasts with a puffed-up chest,
"I've got spiky armor, I'm the best!"
While wrasses giggle at each near miss,
Risky adventures, they reminisce.

Eels tell tales of their slippery plight,
While lanternfish glow, lighting the night.
In the shadows where giggles persist,
Each fish's whimsy plays on the list.

From gobies to groupers, they all convene,
In the abyss, life's a silly routine.
As they spin and twirl in a joke-filled toss,
Survival's a party, no reason to cross!

Beneath the Whispering Waves

In the sea where the fish all boast,
A crab declared he was the most.
With claws held high, he took a stance,
Then tripped on sand and lost his pants!

The jellyfish danced with grace and flair,
While seahorses tangled up in hair.
They giggled loud, their laughter bright,
As dolphins joined in the silly fight!

An octopus managed to juggle fine,
With eight arms flailing, it looked divine.
Yet one slip up, and with a splat,
He knocked a turtle right off his hat!

At sunset's glow, the sea-life cheer,
With fishy tales that we all hold dear.
Under the waves, the laughter sounds,
In this watery world where humor abounds.

A Mosaic of Marine Lives

A clownfish donned a big red nose,
While parrotfish struck ridiculous poses.
Their antics sparked a lively spree,
Turning the sea into a comedy!

A starfish took to the stage one day,
Reciting jokes in a wobbly way.
But when he slipped on a slimy shell,
The punchline got lost in the ocean swell.

The sea cucumber tried to compete,
With a slow dance that was far from fleet.
But the more he swayed, the more they laughed,
As he got tangled with a floating raft!

In this mosaic where life is random,
The undersea comedy finds its fandom.
With giggles and chortles in each tide,
Ocean friends share laughter with pride.

The Ephemeral Bloom

A sea anemone had a beautician's knack,
Painting its tentacles in bright shades of black.
Yet when a fish swam by for a trim,
It accidentally gave him a permanent brim!

A sea urchin tried to host a dance,
Waved its spines, hoping to take a chance.
But when it twirled, it lost its place,
And pricked a clownfish right in the face!

A water lily plopped in for some laughs,
Mountainous in size with oversized gaffs.
When it started to bloom, it opened wide,
And sent a shrimp flying out with pride!

So beware the blooms that are here today,
In this whimsical world that might float away.
With giggles and smiles that fish can't ignore,
Watch for the blooms that bloom evermore!

Ripples of Resilience

A little fish with a brave heart shone,
Swam against waves while all alone.
It shouted, "I can do it, just you wait!"
Then bumped into a rock and shouted, "Fate!"

A turtle tried to race through the blue,
But tripped on seaweed, who knew it too?
He wore a grin, ignoring the fall,
"Hey, look at me! I'm having a ball!"

With a pirate's hat, a pufferfish grinned,
Claiming treasures that he couldn't win.
But when it puffed up in a great display,
All the fish fled shouting, "Not today!"

Yet through the jests and the playful plight,
Life carried on with joy and delight.
In ripples of laughter that echo and sway,
The ocean's resilience is here to stay.

The Coral Symphony

In a world where fish wear shoes,
A clownfish juggles, sharing news.
Turtles twist in fancy hats,
While seahorses dance with acrobats.

The octopus plays a violin,
And all the crabs join in with a grin.
Starfish sing, their voices bright,
What a scene, a pure delight!

The angelfish spin, a dazzling sight,
As jellyfish glide, a sheer delight.
Sharks do the cha-cha, what a show!
Underwater parties, putting on a glow!

With bubbles popping all around,
The fish all cheer, their joy profound.
Lobsters clink their claws in cheer,
As the seaweed sways, oh so dear!

Guardians of the Colors

A parrotfish dons a coat so bright,
While puffers puff, preparing for flight.
Clams wear pearls like crowns so fair,
Who knew the ocean had such flair?

The lionfish struts with princely grace,
While cleaner wrasse tidies up the place.
The hermit crab runs a shell swap shop,
Silly outfits never make him stop!

A grouper grins, a joke in tow,
While blennies gossip, stealing the show.
Dolphins giggle as they play tag,
Under the waves, they're never a drag!

The sea cucumbers dream of fame,
While shells compete in a kickball game.
With laughter echoing through the sea,
These guardians know how to be free!

Tales from the Blue Realm

Once a crab found a shiny thing,
He wore it proudly, began to sing.
Fish laughed hard, their sides did ache,
For that 'treasure' was just a fake!

An octopus tried its hand at art,
Painted with ink, it stole every heart.
While turtles played bingo with style,
Their slow-paced games took a while!

A flounder got tired of being flat,
Tried to be stylish, wore a big hat.
But each time he turned, much to his dread,
He found his fancy hat on his head!

With fish tales told, and laughter shared,
No need for sadness, no one was scared.
Just friends in the blue, in fishy delight,
Making the ocean a pure delight!

Harmonies of the Sea

In a deep sea concert, fish take the stage,
With jellyfish lights, they're all the rage.
The bass guitar's played by a big fat fish,
Everyone's dancing, fulfilling their wish!

With sea urchins keeping the beat so strong,
A beluga sings along, all day long.
A dolphin plays trumpet, blowing sweet sound,
As the crowd waves their fins, joy all around!

The sea anemones sway in delight,
While starfish applaud and cheer with all might.
The mackerel's tumbling adds to the show,
As everyone joins in, a colorful flow!

From the tide pools to depths, the music blares,
With laughter and joy echoing in pairs.
In this underwater concert, a magical spree,
Is life ever dull in the sea? Not a bit, you see!

Mysteries in the Marine Abyss

In the depths where fish do dance,
Octopus wears a fancy pants.
A turtle sings, oh what a sight,
Prawn joins in, hits the high note right.

The clam is clapping, what a show,
Jellyfish wobbles, sways to and fro.
Starfish cheering from their bright thrones,
Sending giggles through the sea's tones.

A crab in shades, he's quite a guy,
Snapping selfies as fish swim by.
A conch, the gossip of the crew,
Tells tall tales of what fish say do.

Oh, those secrets beneath the waves,
Mysteries tickling fins and braves.
In this kingdom of the bright blue sea,
Smile and laugh, it's a fishy spree!

Symphony of the Sea Creatures

A dolphin plays a catchy tune,
To the starry night beneath the moon.
A shrimp thumps on a tiny drum,
The sea is dancing, oh look, here they come!

Squid in stripes bring the trumpet sound,
While seahorses twirl round and round.
A whale belly laughs with a deep bass,
Echoing giggles in this watery space.

Tuna tap dance, flapping their fins,
Mimicking humans with grins and spins.
The bass fish bounces, legs in the air,
It's quite the talent show down there!

As seaweed sways with syncopated beats,
The fish get funky, move their fleets.
Under the waves, a vibrant scene,
A laughter-filled concert, serene and keen!

Tales from the Turquoise Abyss

A flounder claims he's quite the star,
Tells everyone he's traveled far.
With stories of sharks that he did dodge,
His friends just laugh, he's such a mirage.

The anchor fish tell tales of yore,
Of an octopus that wanted to soar.
He tried to glide on bubble gum,
But landed face-first—oh what a bum!

The clownfish giggles, creating pranks,
Dressed as a pirate—swashbuckling flanks.
A battle is brewing, a shrimp with sass,
Squirting water, now who'll be the last?

So gather 'round for stories spun,
In vibrant waters, so much fun.
The turquoise abyss holds laughs galore,
Each creature's antics bring joy to explore!

A Canvas of Crustaceans

A lobster struts in colors bright,
Painting a portrait under moonlight.
Crabs with brushes flailing about,
Creating chaos, that's what they shout.

The shrimp are artists, oh what flair,
Making waves with salty air.
A hermit crab hosts a gallery night,
With shells as frames—oh, what a sight!

But wait! What's this? A seagull swoops,
To steal their masterpiece, oh the goofs!
A chase ensues, legs moving fast,
Art heists in the sea, who'll win? Who'll last?

A canvas of fun, where artists play,
Underneath the shimmering bay.
The crustaceans laugh, it's pure delight,
Creating magic in the soft moonlight!

Life at the Seafloor

In the depths where the sea cucumbers roam,
A crab tells a joke while he makes his new home.
Starfish giggle, forgetting their fate,
They tickle each other; it's a curious slate.

An octopus plays with a lost rubber duck,
Entangled in seaweed, oh what bad luck!
The fish hold their sides as they laugh and they dart,
Planning a party—oh, they're quite the good sport!

A clam sings a ballad, so wildly off-key,
While seahorses dance in a slippery spree.
A whale falls asleep, and the bubble trails pop,
Dreaming of pizza from a magical shop.

At the seafloor circus, the shells take a bow,
Jellyfish juggle, the crowd goes, "Wow!"
This undersea laughter, so bright and so true,
In a world made of wonder, there's always room for two.

A Tapestry of Fins

Fins of the fish create quite the parade,
Dancing through kelp like they're all on a crusade.
A clownfish jokes, wearing stripes that are wild,
While the angelfish giggles, like a luminous child.

A group of small parrotfish munch on some coral,
Complaining of flavors that are too much tooral.
They chat about burgers from the oceanic fair,
And all agree that it would be quite rare.

A lionfish flaunts, with a spiny-bright grin,
Saying, "I'm tougher; let's see you get in!"
But the group of shy blennies just cringe with their fears,
Making a pact to hide out for years.

In this flamboyance, there's laughter and fun,
Each fish with a tale under glittering sun.
As sunlight drapes down, making hues canal,
The tapestry of fins sings of friendship's grand ball.

Ghosts of the Seaweed

In the shadows where the seaweed sways and bends,
A seahorse whispers; it's where laughter blends.
Ghosts of the seaweed have come out to play,
They throw seaweed parties, oh what a display!

A crab in a costume, all dressed as a ghost,
Shares spooky tales with the oyster, his host.
The seaweed all trembles, it's shaking with fear,
But truthfully it's giggling; the jokes are quite clear.

Anemones wiggle; they join in the fun,
Dancing like wild mushrooms, they're hard to outrun!
While hidden in bubbles, the fish hold their sides,
As laughter bubbles up with the oceanic tides.

So when the moon rises, the parties ensue,
With ghosts in the seaweed, you know what to do!
Join in on the laughter, let worries all fade,
In the ghostly seaweed, don't let fun evade.

The Ocean's Canvas

Beneath the blue waves, a painter's delight,
Splashing bright colors, what a beautiful sight!
Clownfish in palettes, they dart here and there,
Creating their art; oh, they do it with flair.

A starfish critiques, with a confident flip,
Saying, "That hue hasn't made quite the trip!"
While dolphins leap in, adding splashes of glee,
It seems every creature is part of this spree.

The brush made of seaweed, so whimsical, true,
Each stroke tells a story, gives life to the blue.
As turtles hold palettes with shells made of gold,
Laughs echo hilariously in legends retold.

So here under water, where colors collide,
An underwater gallery where joy is the guide.
With each stroke a giggle, and laughter so grand,
In the ocean's own canvas, it's all fun unplanned.

Echoes of Endangered Seas

In waters bright with fishy glee,
A turtle lost his way to tea.
He asked a crab which way to go,
Crab replied, "Dude, just take it slow!"

The seahorses danced, oh what a sight,
While octopuses juggled, pure delight.
A dolphin laughed, its jokes not great,
But all agreed, it's worth the wait!

The clowns in fish, with stripes galore,
Performed each night by the sandy shore.
They tickled the seaweed, much to their glee,
"Please don't eat us!" they begged a sea bee.

So in these seas, where laughter's free,
We cherish life and the fishy spree!
Each bubble bursts with giggles and cheer,
Let's raise a fin, let's spread the cheer!

A Voyage Through Sea Gardens

Set sail on waves, a splashy quest,
Where fish don sunglasses, at their best.
Seashells sing with a bubbly sound,
As starfish play hide-and-seek around.

The sea anemones wave and sway,
While clownfish joke the day away.
Grouper plays chess with a curious eel,
Both break for snacks made of seaweed meal.

A jellyfish twirls in a jelly dance,
While crabs try their best to find romance.
They pinch and preen, oh what fun,
"Love in the tide? Come, everyone!"

So gather round in this watery square,
For laughter swims and fills the air.
In gardens deep, the colors glisten,
Join the fun, you won't want to miss 'em!

The Hidden World Below

Beneath the waves, where secrets dwell,
A goldfish tells tales that tickle and sell.
He speaks of pirates, of treasure true,
But mostly of his favorite food, the stew!

An otter spins a yarn so tall,
Of a mermaid's ball and a whale's grand call.
With kelp as decor and crabs as guests,
The party included the ocean's best!

A shy little shrimp kept tapping her feet,
She told a story, oh such a treat!
Of a lobster king with a crown of bling,
Who danced like Jagger and made fish sing.

In this vast blue, such laughter grows,
Where every bubble bursts with prose.
Dive in deep, where stories flow,
The hidden world just loves to show!

Sagas of the Sea Creatures

With gills and fins, they gather 'round,
A sea turtle claims, "I'm ocean-bound!"
While crabs tell tales of sandy delights,
And fish sing songs under moonlit nights.

The squid brings ink for a story grand,
Of a treasure map drawn in the sand.
"Find the X," yells a fish with flair,
But alas, 'twas just a tangle of hair!

A blowfish puffs with exaggerated grace,
"Who's the fairest in this big ol' place?"
The barnacles giggle, stuck as can be,
"Beauty's not found in just you or me!"

So join their banter, so lively and bright,
In the ocean's depths, all fears take flight.
With laughter echoing through every wave,
These sea creatures make us feel so brave!

The Gentle Giants of the Deep

In the deep, where giants glide,
A whale tripped over its own pride.
With a splash and a belly flop,
It created a bubble, a watery pop!

Turtles dance with a slow-motion flair,
Don't ask them to win a race, they wouldn't dare!
They'd rather munch on some seaweed treats,
Than chase after fish with speedy feats.

A squid wearing shades, oh what a sight!
Claiming he's cool, he put up a fight.
But ink clouds and giggles reverberate wide,
As he wipes out while trying to slide!

In this blue world, laughter is free,
With each wiggly critter, there's glee in the sea.
The gentle giants giggle and cheer,
For life underwater is full of good cheer.

Echoes of Underwater Splendor

In a forest of kelp where the dancers sway,
A clam tried to sing but forgot the way.
With notes that were flat and a voice like a croak,
Even the seahorses choked on their joke!

A crab with a hat found it wasn't his style,
He strutted around looking proud for a while.
But hats in the sea don't quite stay put,
He flipped and he flopped, oh boy, what a hoot!

Starfish spin tales of the ocean so grand,
But getting their stories to float is quite planned.
With five arms waving, they tell of great fights,
But really, it's just about dazzling sights!

Echoes of laughter swim through the waves,
With fish telling jokes, oh how the sea saves.
With each giggle and splash, the ocean will tell,
The tales of the deep where the weirdos dwell!

Paintbrushes of the Pacific

With brushes in fins, the fish start to play,
Splashing colors like rainbows, brightening the bay.
A parrotfish giggles, it's quite the artist,
Painting rocks in a swirl, he's the ocean's bravest!

A pufferfish puffs, thinking it's all for show,
But caught in a watercolor, oh no, oh no!
He floats with a gasp, and then he shivers,
Colorful bubbles escape, all over the rivers!

A clownfish juggles shells like a pro,
With a laugh and a flip, it puts on a show.
But juggling in tides, oh friend, what a mess,
When shells turn to soup — now that's just no less!

As the ocean's a canvas, life's splashed wide and free,
Each twist and each turn, brings joy and esprit.
With paintbrushes waving, the sea laughs and thrives,
In this gallery of life, where the funny fish jive!

Cartwheelers of the Current

Twirling and whirling, in currents they spin,
A dolphin goes cartwheeling, "Look at my fin!"
But up in the air, with a flip and a flail,
He dives belly-first — oh what a fail!

Octopuses tango with eight busy feet,
And fish join the dance with a shimmy and beat.
But when scales start to sparkle, they twirl and they trip,
With a flounder so dizzy, it forgets it's a fish!

A school of bright fish in synchronized glee,
Don't ask them to dance, it's a sight we can't see!
They zig and they zag in a bubble-filled spree,
And tumble together in a wave's wild decree!

Cartwheelers of currents, what fun they create,
With each dainty whirl, they can't be late.
With laughter and joy flowing through every tide,
The ocean's just one big carousel ride!

Ballet of the Bright Ones

In the depths, they twirl and spin,
Fins flapping wildly, let the fun begin!
A clownfish slips, oh what a sight,
Dancing with seaweed, lost in delight.

With bubble-blowing moves so grand,
The shrimp tap their toes on the sandy band.
A grouper joins in, with a grin so wide,
Together they frolic, no need to hide!

Their colors flash like a painter's brush,
Creating a canvas in a shimmering rush.
Jellyfish jiggle, gliding with glee,
As the ocean's stage comes alive with spree.

For in this ballet, no one's apart,
Each fish a dancer, with a joyful heart.
Laughter rings through the water so clear,
In a world where the funny is always near.

The Great Blue Gallery

With fishy portraits on the aquarium wall,
Art you can't touch—better not to fall!
A pufferfish puffs, as big as can be,
And says, 'Do I look like a masterpiece to thee?'

A starfish poses, feeling quite grand,
While a sea cucumber sprawls on the sand.
"I've got the flair, and don't need a brush,
Just watch how I wiggle; it's truly a rush!"

Sea turtles float by with artistic aura,
Claiming, "In this gallery, I'm the real flora."
Fish become critics, swimming all around,
Debating the merits of art that they found.

In this underwater space, humor does reign,
Where every odd critter shares in the fame.
The Great Blue Gallery—come take a peek,
Laughter and color make every heart peak!

Legends of the Aquatic Realm

Tales of the sea creatures, stretching long,
Whales sing to fish with a humorous song.
The octopus grins, with eight arms extended,
"This legend of mine? Never quite ended!"

A sea horse prances, dressed in its best,
"I'm the royal heir," it boasts with a jest.
A crab nearby laughs, "Oh what a joke,
You think you're the boss? Just look at my cloak!"

The angelfish shares tales of great feats,
Like swimming through kelp for the finest of treats.
And every sharp tooth from the great barracuda,
Can't match this humor—it's a real shooter!

In this realm where the deep meets the quirky,
Every tale spun is a little bit jerky.
Legends come alive with a wink and a wave,
Where the laughs echo bright, in the ocean they crave!

Dance of the Anemone

Twisting and turning like a soft, plush wave,
Anemones sway—oh, how they behave!
A clownfish arrives, proud as a king,
"Join me, dear friend, let's make this place sing!"

They jiggle with joy, in a rhythm so odd,
While crabs on the sidelines, give a slow nod.
A sea snail attempts to join in the hullabaloo,
But trips on a pebble; oh, boo-hoo!

"Watch this technique!" the anemone sings,
As it waves its fine tentacles—humbly it clings.
"Come on, little fish, do a twirl or a flip,
With my flowy strands, get ready to grip!"

So the dance carries on, a spectacle rare,
With giggles and splashes filling the air.
In the soft embrace of the ocean's delight,
The anemone's dance shines brilliantly bright.

Rainbows at the Bottom

The fish wear suits in colors bright,
They throw a glow that feels just right.
Jellyfish dance like they own the floor,
While crabs tell jokes, who could ask for more?

An octopus plays a game of hide,
In a clam shell, it tries to bide.
Seahorses giggle, flipping with glee,
While starfish roll, as carefree as can be.

Turtles do yoga in coral caves,
Flexing their flippers, oh how they rave!
Clownfish make faces, a comedic delight,
As the sun sets, they party all night.

From the depths of blue, laughs abound,
In this wonderland, joy can be found.
Life below waves, a whimsical sight,
Where every fish prances, glowing with light.

Whirling Vortex of Life

In the spin of a whirlpool, fish take a ride,
Their tails all a-twirl in the ocean's slide.
A dolphin jokes, 'Hold on tight!'
As they swirl and bounce, such a silly sight.

Anemones wave like they're at a show,
While clams shout, 'Bravo!' to the best in the flow.
Sea turtles spin, joining the spree,
Laughing, they say, 'Come whirl with me!'

Starfish stand still, but wish they could glide,
Dreaming of whirlwinds, they can't quite decide.
As the fish swirl by in a dizzying dance,
The seaweed rolls in a green romance.

In this vortex of life, what a vibrant mix,
Fins flapping wildly, performing their tricks.
A parade of laughter, colors collide,
In the ocean's embrace, we take the ride.

Crystalline Companions

The bubbles rise up like pearls of cheer,
Blowing bright giggles from each little sphere.
Tiny fish toss a party sublime,
In crystal-clear waters, they dance to the chime.

Jellybeans swim in their sugary way,
While shrimp play tag in a dazzling ballet.
A clam calls out, 'Join the fun!'
As the light sparkles, we dance, everyone!

Glimmers of laughter in every wave,
A coral party, where we all misbehave.
Octopuses juggle with rocks in the sun,
While laughter erupts, it's a silly run.

In a world of crystals, funny friends thrive,
Every splash brings giggles, so lively, alive!
Together we swirl, in joy we remain,
In this grand underwater, happy domain.

Fauna of Forgotten Reefs

In forgotten nooks, where the reef played coy,
Fish share stories, old tales full of joy.
A grouper grins, 'I once was a star!'
While seahorses whisper, 'We've come so far!'

Crustaceans throw a beach party bash,
Where sea cucumbers join, though they're kind of brash.
Shrimps do the cha-cha on sandy floors,
While conch shells gossip behind closed doors.

A fabled fight broke out one night,
Between gobies and eels, what a comical sight!
With bubbles and giggles, the tales do circulate,
In this playful realm, we all celebrate.

From the depths of obscurity, bright laughter rings,
Where even the dullest sea creatures have flings.
In the fauna's tales, so rich and profound,
Life's a joke here, where joy knows no bounds.

Sunkissed Encounters

In waters bright, where fish do dance,
A starfish waved, 'Hey, give me a chance!'
The clams shut tight, with pearls so grand,
While sea cucumbers, made a rock band.

A turtle in shades, wearing a hat,
Said, "Dive in, folks! Let's have a chat!"
He told fish tales of old sunken ships,
While snails joined in, doing silly flips.

The seahorse twirled in a fancy lace,
As the jellyfish wobbled, keeping the pace.
With a wink and a splash, the octopus led,
A conga line of critters, all twirling their threads.

As bubbles rose high, and laughter rang clear,
The underwater party spread joy and cheer.
With wiggling fins and bubbles of fun,
They danced till the day was finally done.

The Enchanted Tide Pools

In tide pools small, where wonders reside,
A crab in sunglasses took a joyride.
Mussels sang songs, though off-key and loud,
While barnacles cheered, forming a crowd.

A hermit crab bragged of his shiny new shell,
While sea urchins snickered, knowing him well.
A starfish chimed in with a flip and a spin,
"You need a new shell, it's too tight for your chin!"

Anemones waved, like they were in a trance,
As some fish swam by, missing their chance.
The tide whispered secrets, both silly and sweet,
While sand dollars giggled, shaking their feet.

The sea otter rolled, all snug in a pout,
While seaweed played tag, swirling about.
In the pools of delight, where laughter runs free,
The ocean's own carnival, just wait and see!

Odyssey of the Ocean's Palette

In waters so bright, where colors collide,
A parrotfish painted with strokes of great pride.
With brushes of kelp and a splash of pink hue,
He asked, "Do you like it? It's my ocean debut!"

A clownfish chimed in with a jittery zest,
"I prefer stripes! They suit me the best!"
While the nudibranch laughed, multicolored and bold,
Said, "Fashion's an ocean! Don't just do what you're told!"

As bubbles of laughter floated around,
The sea anemone danced in the sound.
A playful pufferfish puffed up with glee,
"Art's in the heart, not just what you see!"

Mollusks held a gallery, with shells stacked just right,
The tide made a canvas, splashed with delight.
In an underwater world where creativity thrived,
With colors and laughter, all art was alive.

Whimsical Worlds Below

Beneath the waves, where silliness reigns,
A fish flapped its fins like it's going insane.
A sea turtle giggled, saying, "Come be my friend!"
While a playful octopus tried to pretend.

With tentacles wiggling, he juggled some shells,
While a clam yelled, "Stop! You're ringing the bells!"
A school of fish munched on popcorn so light,
They laughed at the bubbles that danced in the night.

A dolphin appeared, with a splash and a twirl,
"Who needs a party when you've got a whirl?"
The fish all agreed, and they joined in the fun,
With noodles and giggles, they swam just like one.

In this whimsical world, where oddballs unite,
Underwater shenanigans filled the pure night.
From silly sea dances to pranks that delight,
The ocean's wild laughter echoed, just right.

Stories of the Sea Garden

A clownfish danced in a bright pink house,
Waving at turtles who looked like a mouse.
An octopus juggled with shells and a star,
While seahorses raced in a miniature car.

A crab with a hat made of seaweed so fine,
Declared, 'Come join me for a crabby good time!'
The jellyfish waltzed, doing twirls in the blue,
While all of the fish sang their favorite tune.

The sea cucumber grinned, said, 'Look at me flex!'
As the shrimp cracking jokes made everyone vex.
Laughter erupted from kelp-covered walls,
As fish threw a party, they danced down the halls.

But with a loud splash, the party did fade,
A big whale swam in with a friend, a mermaid!
'Oops!' said the fish, as they scattered in fear,
A lesson was learned: Don't be too sincere!

Echoes of the Ocean Depths

Deep in the blue where the bubblefish roam,
A dolphin told tales of a magical dome.
With the wink of an eye and a flip of its tail,
It led all the fish down a giggling trail.

An eel played guitar while the flounders sang,
In a band made of shells, hear the laughter that rang.
A pirate was lurking, with a parrot so bright,
Who swore the best treasure was a comical sight.

The sea urchins laughed, 'What's the best secret here?'
'It's tickling fish fins that brings such good cheer!'
So they splashed in the waves, a caper so grand,
With a chorus of bubbles, they danced on the sand.

But suddenly came, a hungry old shark,
Who tried to join in, but just made his mark.
The fish rolled in laughter as he swam out of view,
"With moves like that, we don't need a shark stew!"

Tides of Technicolor Dreams

In waters of sorbet, where colors collide,
Lived a fish with a mustache, who swam with great pride.

He hosted a show where starfish would tease,
And seaweed dancers would shimmy with ease.

The anglerfish flickered with a bright little light,
Said, 'Come one, come all, for a fabulous night!'
With music from clams and a conch on the deck,
They partied till sunrise, oh, what a wild wreck!

A pufferfish puffed up, feeling quite bold,
And the crabs, oh dear, would not let him hold!
'We'll see who gets stuck for a real good time!'
As they rolled with the tide, all in rhythm and rhyme.

Yet out from the shadows, a grumpy old stingray,
Called out, 'Stop that ruckus! Please, clear the way!'
But all of the fish burst in playful delight,
Said, 'Oh, don't be such a grouch, join our frolic tonight!'

Secrets of the Sunlit Lagoon

In a lagoon where the sun likes to play high,
Lived a fish with a dream to always fly.
With wings made of bubbles, it soared with great flair,
While seagulls just stared, scratching heads in despair.

A flapper named Fred wore a bright feather hat,
And whispered to all, 'This lagoon? How about that!'
The shrimp threw a bash with a buffet of zest,
Said, 'Join in the fun, it's the finny-fish fest!'

The turtles all laughed at a darning old sting,
Who knitted a scarf, just to show off his bling.
As waves lapped the shore, the sun kissed the sea,
Frogs croaked a tune for the fish jubilee.

But a sneaky old barracuda had plans of his own,
To crash in the party with a mischievous tone.
Yet the fish just ignored him, danced under the sun,
For life in the lagoon was too much fun!

Mysterious Depths

In the depths, where shadows play,
A fish wearing glasses swam all day.
He read a book on seaweed lore,
And laughed at crabs who danced on the floor.

A friendly octopus played with ink,
Leaving messages that made us think.
"Why do we swim in circles so round?"
"Because it's fun to chase your own sound!"

The turtles wore hats, quite a sight,
Complaining about the current's slight bite.
They ordered pizza from a kelp tree,
With extra plankton, it was funny!

A seahorse held a dance-off bright,
But forgot his moves and took flight.
He twirled with glee, a spiraled mess,
Leaving the jellyfish to clean up the stress.

Kingdoms Beneath the Waves

In a kingdom under the gleaming sun,
A crab held court, thinking he'd won.
His throne was made of a soda can,
He declared his reign—"I'm the best, man!"

The dolphins giggled at his grand decree,
Conducting mischief, oh so carefree.
With bubbles they blew, making a fuss,
"We're the real rulers; you're just a plus!"

A clam tried to sing a maritime tune,
But choked on sand and sang to the moon.
His voice was like a rusty door,
Yet, fish all gathered for an encore!

The sea stars twinkled in laughter bright,
As the octopuses plotted a party tonight.
With disco lights made from shiny shells,
They knew it would be a night of tales!

Sunlight's Embrace

Under sunlight, the reef did gleam,
A fish was painting, living the dream.
With an artist's fin and a brush of kelp,
He made a masterpiece, all by himself!

Meanwhile, a turtle in shades reclined,
Sipping on seawater, feeling divine.
"No stress today, just tanning my shell,"
He winked at a crab, who thought he'd yell!

A ray danced by, with moves oh-so bold,
Said, "Join my salsa, come be uncontrolled!"
But the puffer fish puffed up in fright,
"I'll dance in my own way, day or night!"

The bubbles floated, sparkling and bright,
Creating a party that felt just right.
With laughter echoing through watery trails,
Even the seaweed waved with tales!

The Vibrant Tidepool

In a tidepool bustling, full of delight,
A crab in a bowtie gave quite a fright.
He hosted a feast, with snacks galore,
Said, "Take a seat, there's always more!"

A sea star flipped, just trying to dance,
Fell off its rock, without a chance.
The anemones giggled, waving with glee,
"Next time, dear star, don't swing by me!"

An urchin brought cupcakes topped with brine,
"Best dessert ever, don't waste a dime!"
But the seagulls swooped, causing a scene,
And left behind chaos, oh so obscene!

As the tide rolled in, they splashed around,
Creating laughter and joy, unbound.
In this vibrant pool, a lesson we see,
Life's best moments are silly and free!

www.ingramcontent.com/pod-product-compliance
Lightning Source LLC
Chambersburg PA
CBHW051734290426
43661CB00123B/267